Library of Congress Cataloging-in-Publication Data

Verdet, Jean-Pierre.
 The Sky: Stars and Night
illustrated by Christian Broutin, Henri Galeron and
Pierre-Marie Valat; translated by Vicki Bogard
Translation of: Le ciel, les étoiles et la nuit. Includes index.
 Summary: An introduction to the night sky, describing major
constellations and the planets of the solar system.
1. Astronomy — Juvenile literature. [1. Astronomy.]
I. Broutin, Christian, ill. II. Galeron, Henri, ill.
III. Valat, Pierre-Marie, ill. IV. Title.
V. Series: Young Discovery Library; (Series): 32.   90-50776
QB46.V4713   1991   523   ISBN 0-944589-32-4
Printed and bound by L.E.G.O., Vicenza, Italy

CHILDRENS PRESS CHOICE

A Young Discovery Library title selected for educational distribution

ISBN 0-516-08296-5

Written by Jean-Pierre Verdet
Illustrated by Christian Broutin,
Henri Galeron and Pierre-Marie Valat

Specialist Adviser:
Jean-Pierre Verdet,
Astronomer
Paris Observatory

ISBN 0-944589-32-4
First U.S. Publication 1991 by
Young Discovery Library
217 Main St. • Ossining, NY 10562

©*Editions Gallimard, 1987*
Translated by Vicki Bogard
English text © *Young Discovery Library*

The Sky:
Stars and Night

YOUNG DISCOVERY LIBRARY

The sun has just set...
but it is not yet night.
The sky glows, full of colors.
One star is already shining:
we call it the shepherd's star,
but it is not really a star at
all. It is Venus, **a planet...**
like the Earth, where you are
right now, looking at the sky.
Now the pale, mysterious moon
is rising, and soon a whole
skyful of stars will twinkle
and move around the heavens.
Be a stargazer. Will you see
the same stars every night of
the year? The sky is full of
wonders—and secrets.

Constellations: Taurus   Leo

Constellations are groups of stars that make certain forms.

These groups appear year after year, always looking the same. Long ago people gave them names. Do you know Pegasus, Orion or the Big Dipper? The best-known constellations are those the Earth passes in the course of a year: they form **the zodiac**. Astrologers think these stars rule our lives, many others do not believe that can be so. But you will find Astrology columns in your daily newspapers, giving lots of advice.

There are twelve constellations in the zodiac. The Earth takes twelve months to pass them. Here are their names and symbols—things people thought they looked like:

Gemini	Aquarius	Libra
Taurus	Capricorn	Virgo
Aries	Sagittarius	Leo
Pisces	Scorpio	Cancer

Can you find the Big Dipper?

The Big Dipper is a large constellation made up of seven stars. Three of them form a broken line, the other four a rectangle: they look like a dipper. The edge of the dipper points the way to the North Star, about four "dippers" higher. The North Star is the star around which all the other stars seem to move. It shows you which way is North. You can also find it at the end of the Little Dipper's handle.

Little Dipper

Big Dipper

The Big and Little Dippers travel around the North Star every night like the hands of a clock going backwards. The stars keep moving, even in the daytime.

The Earth turns while circling the sun.

How does the Earth move?

The stars seem to move around the North Star. The Sun *seems* to rise every morning, move across the sky, and set in the evening. That is because the Earth is spinning like a top. The Earth's **axis** crosses the sky near the North Star. The Earth completes one **rotation** in twenty-four hours, but that is not all the traveling it does: in one year it also circles the sun!

So, it may not feel like the Earth is moving, but we are spinning and racing through space! The first person to prove that was Copernicus, over 400 years ago.

**We have always
dreamed of walking
on the moon!**
Ever since we have
gazed up at the sky,
the moon has fascinated
us. Some people imagined
that there was "a man in the
moon." Promising someone
the moon meant promising them
the impossible. Then one day
in 1969 the astronaut, Neil
Armstrong, took "one small step
for a man, one giant step for
mankind."
To achieve that step took
almost ten years and billions
of dollars, to make the machines
and train the people involved.

Without the sun, we couldn't see the moon! The moon gives off no light of its own. It shines with light from the sun. When the moon is full, you can see spots on its surface. The dark spots are called **seas**—even though there is no water on the moon! These "seas" are really large plains, covered with gray dust. The light colored spots are **mountains**, very high and jagged. If you look at the moon with a pair of good binoculars, you will see that its surface is covered with furrows, grooves and holes of all sizes.

The moon is much smaller than the Earth. It has a diameter about one-fourth of the Earth's.

The moon's changing appearance.

The moon revolves around the Earth. If the moon had its own light, it would always look **full** to us. But the moon, like the Earth, is lit by the sun. At times we can see all or only part of it lit up. This is caused by its position in relation to the Earth. When the moon is between the Earth and the sun, we cannot see it at all! The different aspects of the moon are called **lunar phases.**

If we lived on the moon, we would see the phases of the Earth. Here is how it would look.

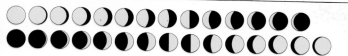

Here are all the phases of the moon. They take 29½ days, one lunar month, from start to finish, nearly a calendar month.

Look carefully at this drawing. Imagine the sun is to the right of this book. You are on Earth (1) in the drawing's middle. Note each position of the moon in relation to the Earth (2) and you will understand the phases of the moon (3). Remember, when you look towards the top, the sun is on the right. It's on the left when you look towards the bottom.

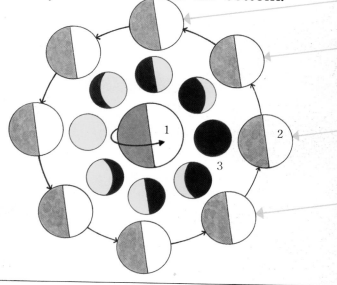

The moon is opposite the sun. We see all of it lit up.
It is highest at midnight: the moon is full.

Four days later, it doesn't reach its highest point
until 3 a.m. It is no longer full.

Eight days later, the moon is in its last quarter.
It rose one hour ago. It is now 2 a.m.

It is 8 a.m. The moon is getting thinner. By the
time it reaches its highest point, the sun will hide it.

This is the new moon. It reaches its highest point
with the sun at noon, but we cannot see it at all.

Five days later: the moon has moved away from the sun.
We can see it once again. It is 7 p.m. Soon it will set.

The moon slowly enters the Earth's shadow.
It grows darker, then disappears for a moment.

When the moon disappears!

Month after month, the Earth and
the moon play hide-and-seek.
Since the Earth is lit by the sun
it has its own shadow—just like
yours on a sunny day. In this
game the moon sometimes moves into
the Earth's shadow. The shadow
takes a nibble, then a big bite.
Soon the moon disappears. Long
ago people thought a dragon was
gobbling it up!
But don't worry. The moon will
return: it was only an **eclipse.**
There is about one lunar
eclipse per year.

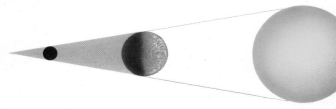

moon   Earth   sun

24

The Earth is not the only planet that orbits the sun! There is the moon and eight other planets.
Some are as small as the Earth. They have surfaces hard enough to run on: Mercury, Venus, Mars and Pluto. The others are much bigger and are gaseous, not solid. Those are Jupiter, Saturn and its rings, Uranus and Neptune.

From left to right after the sun: Mercury, Venus, the Earth, Mars, Jupiter, Saturn, Uranus, Neptune and Pluto. Their size ratio is correct, but to show you their relative distance from the sun, this book would have to be a mile wide!

All the planets, like the Earth and the moon, are lit by the sun's rays.
Between Mars and Jupiter, there are also many tiny "planets" in orbit. They are perhaps pieces of a planet that exploded.

The sky's surprises

The sky's good order may be disturbed by **comets and meteorites.** Comets are little glowing balls with long tails of gas.

Meteorites this big are very rare. In 1908 a giant meteorite destroyed a forest almost 40 miles wide in eastern Siberia.

They come from the far reaches of the solar system. They pass near us and continue on their way. Meteorites are the rocks of the solar system. When one passes near the Earth, it is pulled into our atmosphere. It falls and usually burns up. What do we call the glowing path of this fall? A falling star!

The Meteor Crater in Arizona. Its 4,200 foot diameter was created by a meteorite which fell less than 100,000 years ago.

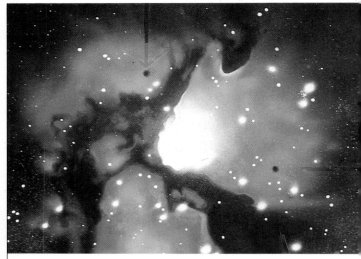

Stars are often born together in gigantic clouds of hydrogen. In the Universe, stars are constantly being born. We can see stars forming in the Trifid Nebula, but only with a very powerful telescope.

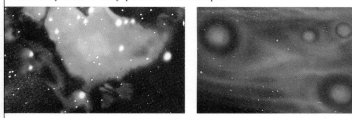

Stars are born. A cloud of gas and dust begins to contract, producing one or more stars.

The more a cloud contracts, the more the gases inside heat up. Then the star will begin to shine.

How do stars live and die?

Stars are enormous balls of hot gas. They give off their own light. But they do not burn as coal does. They transform their main gas, hydrogen, into another gas, helium. This change gives off heat for billions of years. **But stars do eventually die:** if they are very big, they explode. If they are smaller, they cool down too much.

The sun is our star.

It is a medium-sized star in the middle of its life. It has been burning for about five billion years. In another five billion years, it will die.

Once a star has burned up its hydrogen, it first expands and becomes a red giant. Then it collapses and becomes a white dwarf.

Observe the southern sky in the winter.

Observe the southern sky in the summer.

Discovering the sky

If you want to observe the stars,
pick a clear, moonless night.
Otherwise, the moonlight would
make it hard to see them.
You can bring binoculars but if
you don't have any, there are
still 2,500 stars you can see
with the naked eye!

If you observe the southern sky
in the winter, you might see
these constellations:

1. Orion
2. Taurus
3. The Pleaides
4. Perseus
5. Aries
6. Auriga
7. Andromeda
8. Pegasus
9. Pisces
10. Aquarius
11. Cetus
12. Eridanus

In the summer, you can see these
constellations in the sky:

1. Lyra
2. Hercules
3. Ophiucus
4. Corona Borealis
5. Bootes
6. Virgo
7. Libra
8. Sagittarius
9. Capricorn
10. Aquarius
11. Pisces
12. Pegasus
13. Delphinus
14. Aquila
15. Cygnus
16. Serpens
17. Scorpio

This telescope is used
to observe stars
invisible to the naked eye.

Here is our galaxy, the Milky Way, seen from the side.

The sun, our star, is not alone in the **Universe.** It belongs to an immense wheel containing millions of stars.
It is the Galaxy. It rotates, carrying us in a full circle once every 250 million years. You didn't know the Earth was going for such a long ride! The Universe appears to be full of millions upon millions of galaxies. Most of these group together, like stars and planets. In the Universe, there are also great clouds of gas and dust. They shine with light from the stars. An example of this is the Trifid Nebula.

If we could climb high above our Galaxy to get a good look at it, we would see it like this one, the Whirlpool galaxy in Canes Venatici.

Ptolemy, Greek astronomer
200 A.D.

Copernicus, Polish astronomer
1473-1543

Kepler, German astronomer
1571-1630

Galileo, Italian astronomer
1564-1642

Newton, English mathematician
1643-1727

Einstein
1879-1955

Giants of astronomy.

We have taken a long time to understand even a little about the sky. These are some astronomers who have made great leaps.

Ptolemy lived in Alexandria. He believed the Earth was the center of the Universe. His book on astronomy, the Almagest, was unchallenged for 1500 years.

Copernicus rejected Ptolemy's thinking. He said that the Earth rotates once every 24 hours and orbits the sun in one year, making it like the other planets.

Kepler discovered that planets move in ellipses, not circles. He gave us their principles of movement.

Galileo was the first to use a telescope to observe the sky, in 1609. A whole new world became visible: Jupiter's satellites, lunar mountains, and Saturn's rings.

Newton was a mathematician, physicist, chemist and astronomer. He discovered the laws of gravity, which makes apples fall from trees and the moon orbit the Earth, among other things.

Einstein is the most famous scientist of the 20th century. German-born, he fled to the United States to escape Nazi persecution. By discovering the Theory of Relativity, he revolutionized our view of the world, from the largest things to the smallest. For example, the speed at which a clock runs depends on how fast it is moving. It will not be the same in a speeding rocket as it is on Earth.

The Night Is a Big Black Cat

The Night is a big black cat
    The Moon is her topaz eye,
The stars are the mice she hunts at night,
    In the field of the sultry sky.

               G. Orr Clark

THE STARS

  What do the stars do
    Up in the sky,
Higher than the wind can blow,
    Or the clouds can fly?

Each star in its own glory
    Circles, circles still;
As it was lit to shine and set,
    And do its Maker's will.

             Christina Rossetti

Index

Books of Discovery for children five through ten...

Young Discovery Library is an international undertaking — the series is now published in nine countries. It is the world's first pocket encyclopedia for children, 120 titles will be published.

Each title in the series is an education on the subject covered: a collaboration among the author, the illustrator, an advisory group of elementary school teachers and an academic specialist on the subject.

The goal is to respond to the endless curiosity of children, to fascinate and educate.

For a catalog of other titles,
please write to: Young Discovery,
             P.O. Box 229,
             Ossining, NY 10562